Presented to

_____

by_____

on_____

Visit Tyndale's website for kids at www.tyndale.com/kids.

TYNDALE and *Little Blessings* are registered trademarks of Tyndale House Publishers, Inc. The Little Blessings characters are a trademark of Elena Kucharik.

The Tyndale Kids logo is a trademark of Tyndale House Publishers, Inc.

Easter Stories and Prayers

First printing by Tyndale House Publishers, Inc., in 2015.

Designed by Jacqueline L. Nuñez

ISBN 978-1-4964-0280-6

For manufacturing information regarding this product, please call 1-800-323-9400.

Printed in China

21 20 19 18 17 16 15
7   6   5   4   3   2   1

Little Blessings Easter Stories and Prayers

Kathleen Long Bostrom | Illustrated by Elena Kucharik

TYNDALE KIDS

Tyndale House Publishers, Inc.
Carol Stream, Illinois

little Blessings®

Why is There a Cross?

Kathleen Long Bostrom | Illustrated by Elena Kucharik

When I am in church
and I look all around,
I always try hard
not to make any sound.

I see on the wall,
from the place where I sit,
A very large cross,
and it scares me a bit.

I know that when Jesus
    was ready to die,
He died on a cross,
    but I'm wondering, *Why?*

What did he do
    that was so very wrong?
Why couldn't everyone
    just get along?

Did Jesus feel sad?
    Do you think he was scared?
I wonder, *Did Jesus*
    think nobody cared?

Why did his life
    have to turn out this way?
Could Jesus have changed it
    by running away?

How can I manage
    to do my own part
To show I love Jesus
    with all of my heart?

            You're wanting to know
                what the cross is about?
            It isn't so easy
                to figure it out.

                    Let's look through the Bible,
                        for then we will see
                    Why the cross is important
                        to you and to me.

The crosses we see—
    both the large and the small—
Remind us that Christ
    gave his life for us all.

His death on the cross
was a part of the plan
That God had in mind
when Creation began.

Romans 3:23; 7:19-20; Matthew 26:53-54; Colossians 2:13-14

Although we may struggle
   with all of our might,
There's simply no way
   we will always do right.

      Jesus was willing
         to die for our sin.
      He gave up his life
         so that we can all win!

19

Hebrews 7:25-26; 1 Peter 2:22; Romans 6:6, 18; Psalm 34:1

Jesus is perfect—
    as good as can be.
He went to the cross
    so that we could be free:

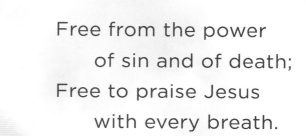

Free from the power
of sin and of death;
Free to praise Jesus
with every breath.

21

Even though Jesus
    did just what God asked,
Facing the cross
    was a difficult task.

Just before Jesus
    was taken away,
He went to a garden
    and knelt down to pray.

He said with great sadness,
    "Dear God, help me through.
You know that I'll do
    what you ask me to do."

Jesus could face, then,
    what had to be done.
He knew that God loved him,
    for he is God's Son.

He went to the cross:
    On Good Friday he died.
A few of his friends
    were right there by his side.

Although it is sad
   that our Lord had to die,
Christ rose from the dead,
   and that isn't a lie!

Matthew 28:5-6; Acts 2:24; Colossians 1:22; Romans 3:22

Because Jesus lives,
      we can share in his glory,
And this is the truth
      of the whole Easter story!

The cross, which was once
     such a terrible sight,
Now shines with the beauty
     of God's holy light.

If you trust in Jesus
     and give him your best,
You'll show that you love him,
     and you will be blessed.

Nothing can keep you
    apart from God's love;
No, nothing on earth
    or in heaven above.

Death cannot stop it,
    not worry or fear.
God's love is forever,
    so be of good cheer!

little Blessings®

Who Is Jesus?

Kathleen Long Bostrom | Illustrated by Elena Kucharik

Dear Jesus, please show me,
for I want to see
The ways you're the same
and yet different from me.

I'd like to know what
you were like as a boy.

Did you have a favorite
story or toy?

Did you take a short nap
when you needed to rest?

Were there special people
that you liked the best?

And what kinds of food
    did you most like to eat?
I think I could live
    on just ice cream and sweets!

What made you feel happy?
    And what made you mad?
Was there ever a time
    when you felt really sad?

Did you always take time
to pray every day?
When you talked to God,
tell me, what did you say?

I feel so unhappy
that you had to die.
Oh, why did that happen
to you, Jesus? Why?

I'M JESUS, GOD'S SON,
and I want you to see
The Bible can teach you
a lot about me.

I came from my Father
to show you the way
To live as God wants you
to live every day.

Luke 1:35; John 1:1

I came to the earth
as a baby, like you,
So you have a birthday,
and I have one too!

I came down from heaven
as God's only Son
To show all the world
that God loves everyone.

There isn't much written
to help you to know
Just what I was like
as a boy long ago.

I was, in some ways,
just like all other kids.
I played, and I thought
about things like they did.

The time hurried past,
   as I grew and I grew.
God loved me, and so did
   the people I knew.

I changed through the years
from a boy to a man.
My life all along
was a part of God's plan.

I loved to tell stories
    to any who'd hear,
While people would gather
    from far and from near.

They followed me closely
wherever I led,
So eager to hear
every word that I said.

I traveled a lot,
    walking mile after mile.
And when I got tired,
    I would sleep for a while.

One time when I just
    couldn't wait for a bed,
I curled up and slept
    in a rowboat instead.

I picked out twelve friends
    who would travel with me
Wherever God sent me,
    on land and on sea.

John 15:12, 14; 6:11; Matthew 6:31-33

You, too, are my friends
if you do as I do
And love one another
as I have loved you.

I liked to eat fish,
and I liked to eat bread.
I made sure that those
who were with me were fed.

So don't fret about
what you'll eat or you'll wear.
My Father will help you,
for he really cares.

I felt all the very same
feelings you feel.
The joy that I have
for my people is real.

I spoke out in anger
at people who lied;
I cried when I heard
that a good friend had died.

I prayed to my Father
in good times and bad.
He listened to every
concern that I had.

Luke 24:46; John 16:23-24; 10:18; 3:17

When you pray to God,
    you should pray in my name,
For my love and God's love
    are one and the same.

I died on a cross
    so that others could live
And know there is nothing
    that God can't forgive.

The day that I died
    was a sad one, but then
God gave me a new life.
    Now I live again!

I'm just like a lamp
glowing softly with light.
So you can feel safe
in the dark of the night.

But sometimes my love
is as bright as the sun
That shines like it has
since the world was begun.

Matthew 5:14-16; 28:19-20

So if you are willing,
  please come, follow me.
Then you'll be my light
  and will help people see

That God's love is so great,
  it will never run out.
Now that is good news
  to tell others about!

little Blessings®

What is Prayer?

Kathleen Long Bostrom | Illustrated by Elena Kucharik

I have a few questions
    to ask about prayer:
Can I talk to God
    anytime, anywhere?

Are there special words
    I should use when I pray?
Should I pray at nighttime
    or during the day?

Does God hear the prayers
    that I don't even speak?
How many times
    may I pray in one week?

When I say my prayers,
    should I bow down my head
And kneel on my knees
    by the side of the bed?

69

When I first begin,
    do I call God by name?
Should all of my prayers
    be exactly the same?

Does God keep a list
    of my prayers from before?
Will God give me all
    that I ask for and more?

Can I pray to God
    when I'm angry inside?
Or would it be better
    to go off and hide?

Can I pray for things
   like a toy or a bike?
Should I pray for people
   I don't even like?

Can I pray for something
and then pray again?
Why do we have to
end up with "amen"?

You want to know more
about how you should pray?
God's answer to that is,
"Terrific! Hooray!"

The Bible will tell you
just what you should know.
Let's see what it says to us—
ready, set, GO!

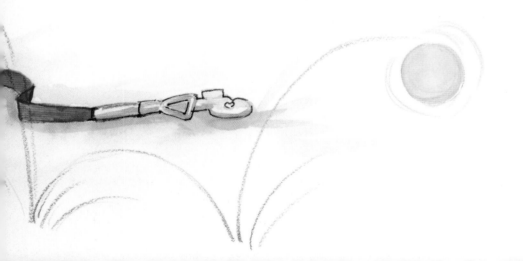

Talking to God
is a great thing to do.
And God's always ready
to listen to you.

You don't have to carefully
    choose every word.
But you can be sure
    that your prayers will be heard.

For even before
    you have started to pray,
God already knows
    what you're going to say!

Pray all you want to—
    it's never too much.
Prayer is the way
    you and God keep in touch.

Although you should always
    say thank you and please,
You really don't have to
    get down on your knees.

You can sit when you pray,
     or lie down in your bed.
You can keep your eyes open
     and stand on your head!

It's never a problem
     however you start.
But God really wants you
     to pray from your heart.

The more that you pray,
      the more often you'll find
That prayers are all different,
      not all the same kind.

There are prayers of thanksgiving
and also of praise,
Like, "Thank you, dear God,
for your wonderful ways!"

1 John 1:9; Psalm 66:18-19

When you have done something
    that you know is wrong,
Ask God to forgive you—
    it doesn't take long.

If you're truly sorry,
    then God will forgive.
And this will be true
    for as long as you live.

When you are afraid
    or you're grouchy or blue,
Then talking to God
    is the best thing to do!

You can pray to the Lord
    for whatever you need.
But praying for others
    is special indeed.

Matthew 5:44-45; Mark 11:24-25; Proverbs 15:8; Colossians 3:17

Praying for someone
who isn't your friend
Is good for that person—
and you, in the end.

By praying for people
to know of God's love,
You're God's little blessing—
a gift from above.

God's answers to prayers
    may come fast or come slow.
But God always answers,
    and that much we know.

God never forgets
    what you've asked for before.
But God doesn't mind
    if you want to talk more.

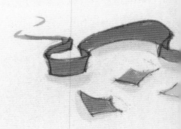

Ending your prayer
   with "amen" is a way
Of saying, "I've finished
   my prayer now, okay?"

A prayer is a lot
    like a telephone call.
You talk and you listen,
    but that isn't all.

There's no busy signal—
    you'll always get through.
And God never, ever
    will hang up on you!

What About Heaven?

Kathleen Long Bostrom | Illustrated by Elena Kucharik

I know that God loves me.
Of this there's no doubt.
But what about heaven?
What's that all about?

Is heaven a place
that is near or that's far?
Can I get to heaven
by boat or by car?

How will I find it?
  Who'll show me the way?
Does heaven have nighttime?
  And what about day?

Can I have a room
  that is only for me?
Do I have to pay,
  or can I stay for free?

Will I look the very
  same way I do now?
Will everyone know
  who I am? If so, how?

What food will I eat?

   And what clothes will I wear?

When I get to heaven,

   who else will be there?

Does heaven have mountains,
and trees I can climb?
What will I do there
with all of my time?

109

Is there enough space
 for the animals, too?
Will there be some kind
 of a heavenly zoo?

Since God is in heaven,
 it has to be great.
Can I go there now,
 or do I have to wait?

111

All questions have answers,
    but some you won't learn
Till God says it's time
    for his Son to return.

Your questions are good ones,
so let's dive right in
And see what the Bible says.
Ready? Begin!

Though heaven's a place
    that you can't see from here,
It says in the Bible
    that heaven is near.

You don't need to know
    how to fly or to swim.
The way is with Jesus,
    believing in him.

It always is daytime—
  there never is night.
The light of God's love
  will be shining so bright.

Jesus will give you
  a room of your own,
With others nearby
  so you won't feel alone.

Your body will change
  so it's perfect and new,
And yet you will still be
  the very same you.

1 Corinthians 15:42, 44; Isaiah 29:18; 30:29; 40:31

But here's something different,
and this is no trick:
In heaven nobody
will ever get sick!

Our hurts will be healed,
and the deaf will all hear.
The blind will see clearly.
There's nothing to fear!

Everyone there
will be able to talk,
To sing and to dance,
and to run and to walk.

In heaven God serves you
the very best meal.
You'll never be hungry—
now that's a good deal!

The clothes that you'll wear
will be white and so clean;
In heaven you won't need
a washing machine!

Even the animals
won't want to fight;
They'll all get along—
they will not scratch or bite.

Though time has no ending,
    you'll never get bored;
For thousands of years
    seem like days to the Lord.

Heaven is full
    of such beautiful things:
The music of millions of
    angels who sing.

Rivers like crystal
    and seas smooth as glass,
Emeralds glowing
    like green springtime grass.

Mountains and jewels
    of every type,
Trees full of fruits
    that are juicy and ripe.

Sadness and pain
    will be taken away;
Once you are there,
    you'll be happy to stay.

All of God's children,
the young and the old,
Will gather together
on streets made of gold.

And then there will be
such a grand celebration
When heaven and earth
have become one creation!

Life will be perfect,
for heaven's the place
We'll see God, the Father
and Son, face-to-face.

For God will be there,
everywhere that you are;
And Jesus will shine
like a bright morning star.

Heaven is wonderful,
don't you agree?
It's simply the best place
we ever could be!

About the Author
Kathleen Long Bostrom is the author of more than a dozen children's books, which have sold well over one million copies. Kathy earned a master of arts in Christian education and a master of divinity from Princeton Theological Seminary, and a doctor of ministry in preaching from McCormick Theological Seminary. Kathy and her husband, Greg, live in Illinois, and they have three children.

About the Illustrator
Elena Kucharik, well-known Care Bears artist, has created the Little Blessings characters that appear in the line of Little Blessings products for young children and their families. For more than twenty-five years Elena has been a freelance illustrator. During this time she was the lead artist and developer of Care Bears, as well as a designer and an illustrator for major corporations and publishers. Elena and her husband live in Connecticut and have two grown daughters.

Books in the Little Blessings line

CP0216